The Quick and Easy Guide to Mind Map

*Improve Your Memory,
Be More Creative,
and Unleash Your Mind's Full Potential*

Thomas C. Randall

www.ImproveYourMemoryToday.net

Copyright Notice

Copyright © 2012 by Thomas C. Randall. All Rights Reserved.

Reproduction or translation of any part of this work beyond that permitted by section 107 or 108 of the 1976 United States Copyright Act without permission of the copyright owner is unlawful. Requests for permission or further information should be addressed to the author.

Thomas C. Randall
www.ImproveYourMemoryToday.net

This publication is designed to provide accurate and authoritative information in regard to the subject matter covered. It is sold the understanding that the publisher is not engaged in rendering legal, accounting, or other professional services. If legal advice or other expert assistance is required, the services of a competent professional person should be sought.

First Printing, 2012

ISBN-13: 978-1478190660

ISBN-10: 1478190663

Printed in the United States of America

Liability Disclaimer

The Publisher has strived to be as accurate and complete as possible in the creation of this book, notwithstanding the fact that he does not warrant or represent at any time that the contents within are accurate due to the rapidly changing nature of the market in general.

While all attempts have been made to verify information provided in this publication, the Publisher assumes no responsibility for errors, omissions, or contrary interpretation of the subject matter herein. Any perceived slights of specific persons, peoples, or organizations are unintentional.

In practical advice books, like anything else in life, there are no guarantees of results. Readers are cautioned to reply on their own judgment about their individual circumstances to act accordingly.

This book is not intended for use as a source of legal, business, accounting or financial advice. All readers are advised to seek services of competent professionals in legal, business, accounting, and finance field.

By reading this book, you assume all risks associated with using the advice given below, with a full understanding that you, solely, are responsible for anything that may occur as a result of putting this information into action in any way, and regardless of your interpretation of the advice.

Foreword

This book is a compact yet comprehensive handbook on one of the most powerful thinking tools—Mind Map. You might have picked up this book without knowing what Mind Map is or with some background knowledge. Either way, I think you will find something valuable in this book.

If you have no prior experience with this tool, this book will provide you with everything you need to get started with this wonderful tool. If you have been using this tool in your life for some time, on and off, you will find ways to fully leverage the power of Mind Map.

Also, unless you are someone who is an expert Mind Mapper and owns high-end Mind Mapping software programs, you will gain new insight how Mind Map fits in the context of today's fast developing technology, which is hard to find in other books on Mind Map.

While Mind Map is a great tool in itself for leveraging your mental capacity, if you are interested in developing your memory for the long haul and unleashing your full mental potential, you might want to check out my other books:

The Quick and Easy Guide to Memory Improvement: 45 Practical Tips You Can Use to Boost Your Memory
(details: improveyourmemorytoday.net/book)
The Quick and Easy Guide to Mnemonics: Improve Your Memory Instantly with 15 Powerful Memory Aids
(details: improveyourmemorytoday.net/book2)

    They cover a lot of ground in the subject of memory improvement, and show you practical steps you can take to build your memory both short- and long-term.
    I will greatly appreciate it if you can let me know what you thought about this book, how helpful it was, any improvements or suggestions to make this book better, or anything. If you liked the book, or if you didn't, let me know via emailing info@ImproveYourMemoryToday.net or by leaving a review on the Amazon website. You can also get more information on www.ImproveYourMemoryToday.net.
    Again, thank you for purchasing this guide, and I hope you enjoy your reading!

Thomas C. Randall

Table of Contents

Foreword .... **ix**

Chapter 1. What Is Mind Map? **1**

How it works *2*

Key features & characteristics *3*

Benefits of Mind Map *7*

Some caveats of Mind Map *9*

Other methods of visual diagramming *12*

Chapter 2. How to Draw a Mind Map

(: the quickest and easiest description you'll ever see) **15**

Chapter 3. How to Personalize a Mind Map
.... **21**

Color *22*

Size *22*

Shapes *24*

Lines or shapes? *24*

Symbol *25*

Images *26*

Different line shapes *26*

Overall layout of the Mind Map *27*

Chapter 4. Potential Uses of Mind Map ... **29**

Brainstorming *30*

Creative writing *34*

Organizing information *38*

Note taking *39*

Study/learning *43*

Presentation *46*

Problem solving *47*

Systematic design *49*

Chapter 5. Mind Map on a Computer 53

Computerized vs. hand-written Mind Map. *54*

Potential usages for computer-based Mind Map *60*

A list of Mind Map software *63*

Chapter 6. How to take it a step further 65

In Closing… *70*

Appendix.. **73**

List of Mind Mapping Software *73*

Reference *76*

Chapter 1.
What Is Mind Map?

Mind Map is a diagram used to visually portray the relationship and connection between ideas, words or other items around a central idea or key word. Other names of Mind Map include "spidergram". Mind Mapping was brought to the mainstream by British Author Tony Buzan in the 1970s. Although the modern Mind Map is by far the most popular method of visually representing thoughts and words, it is not the first visual diagram ever existed. Early forms of visual diagram of mental construct dates back to 4C, where Greek philosopher Porphyry of Tyre used a diagram to summarize Aristotle's ideas.

Mind Map, according to its protagonist Tony Buzan, is very powerful because it visually portrays what's in your mind. By putting down the concepts inside your head and how they are linked on a paper, you can better understand both the macro-(overall picture) and the micro-(on a small scale) structure of a particular thought system. Thus, the name "Mind Map": it maps out your mind. We will discuss more on the benefits of Mind Mapping shortly.

How it works

Let's look at an example of a Mind Map first.

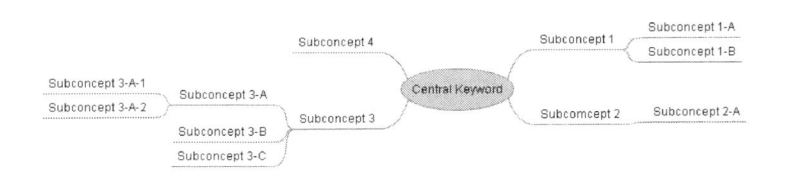

```
                                          Subconcept 1-A
                   Subconcept 4    Subconcept 1
                                          Subconcept 1-B
Subconcept 3-A-1
                Subconcept 3-A    Central Keyword
Subconcept 3-A-2                       Subcomcept 2    Subconcept 2-A
                  Subconcept 3
            Subconcept 3-B
            Subconcept 3-C
```

Mind Map is consisted of three simple elements: a central concept or keyword, subconcepts or keywords, and the lines connecting them. The central concept or keyword is the "theme" of that Mind Map. Everything on the Mind Map is related to that central concept in some way. Then, as you can see on the example, subconcepts that are immediately related to the central concept are connected to it, then, sub-subconcepts that are related to each subconcept are connected to the respective keywords. This results in a radial structure, where the keywords radiate from one central idea. As you will see in the following chapters, there are no hard-and-fast rules for drawing a Mind Map, other than having one central keyword and using lines to "branch out" ideas from that keyword. There are no limits to how many keywords or different levels of them you can write.

Of note, I've used the words "subconcepts" and "sub-subconcepts" only to make the explanation easier: the concepts need not be related in a hierarchical manner. They are "sub" and "sub-sub" only in the context of the central key idea. As you can later see in this book, the sub-or sub-sub-concepts can become the central keyword for another Mind Map.

Key features & characteristics

Here are some key features of Mind Map:
- Visual
- Multi-dimensional
- Radial / centralized
- Association-based
- Clustered
- Keyword-oriented
- Flexible

Let's explore each of these characteristics briefly.

a. Visual

As mentioned earlier, Mind Map is a method of visually representing the relationship of concepts. As humans are primarily visual creatures, it enhances the comprehension and retention of the material. This is helped by not only the organized and hierarchical structure but also other visual elements you can add to the Mind Map, such as color, symbols and pictures. Also, a well-drawn Mind Map enables you to understand the overall structure faster and more clearly.

   b. Multi-dimensional

     I'll explain it in terms of note taking, which was the primary use of Mind Map when it first came out. (However, Mind Map is so much more than a clever note taking method. You'll understand what I mean by the end of this book).

     Traditional note-taking relies on the chronological order in which the material is presented, with no other way of describing how the parts relate to each other. It is fundamentally one-dimensional. However, Mind Map utilizes a two-dimensional space to explore an idea multi-dimensionally. Typically, the ideas in a Mind Map are arranged on multiple levels, and one idea is connected to many. Also, each idea is connected to all the other ideas with various levels of separation (how many "levels" or different keywords there are between them). Therefore, this innate multi-dimensionality gives Mind Map a considerable advantage over traditional note taking or other methods of organizing your thought, because you can get both the detailed relationships and the birds-eye view of a subject.

   c. Radial / centralized

Chapter 1. What Is Mind Map?

This is a unique characteristic of Mind Map. Unlike visual diagrams such as concept map, Mind Map has *one* central idea from which other ideas are mapped out radially. While this characteristic isn't something that makes Mind Map superior in itself over other visual diagrams, it has certain advantages. First, it provides an overarching theme for the whole map. Second, it enables you to explore a single concept in depth. Third, it shows you how close or distant an idea is to the central concept by how close or far away it is to/from the center of a Mind Map, where the central concept is written down.

d. Association-based

One of the key elements of Mind Map is the connection or association between the concepts. This is probably the biggest difference from the traditional linear way of organizing and presenting information. Although some other variations of visual map, which I will discuss in a moment, might portray every existing connection between different items in a decentralized fashion, Mind Map does it in a unique way; how they relate to the central keyword (resulting from the previous feature). Often times the connections between elements that are not a part of the characteristic radial branching scheme is minimized or omitted. This has in part to do with the next feature which is called clustering.

e. Clustering

There are multiple levels in a Mind Map and the subtopics work as a node. As you can see, the centralized and radial nature of Mind Map makes the relationship of the keywords essentially one-to-many; the central keyword is connected to many sub-keywords, which in turn are connected to their sub-keywords and so on. Therefore, a Mind Map becomes a collection of clusters across multiple levels. This is the feature that allows for both macro- and micro- level thinking with Mind Map. You can think of the whole Mind Map as one big cluster of ideas and keywords, or focus on a sub-cluster of that for a more detailed insight.

f. Keyword-oriented

More often than not Mind Map contains one word or a short phrase with few words for each entry. Tony Buzan even insists that you only write one keyword per entry. Whether you use a single word or a short phrase, this makes Mind Map compact and concise in nature. By representing each idea with a keyword or two, you inevitably focus on the core of that idea, leaving out unnecessary or superfluous parts. Consequently, you can fit more ideas in the same amount of space, plus the relationship between them. If the keywords are selected wisely, the Mind Map alone can act as a cue of the ideas for you, which will have an effect of improved memory and more effective learning/studying.

Chapter 1. What Is Mind Map?

g. Flexible

Mind Map is very flexible and customizable in nature. There are no rules set in stone about how you should draw a Mind Map, other than that you need to have one idea and connect the ideas with a line. You can use different colors, shapes, symbols, images, and other tricks as your imagination allows. Given these possibilities, you are free to experiment and find a combination of these that works best for you. You will learn how to customize a Mind Map for you in Chapter 3.

Also, the advent of computerized Mind Mapping software has made it ever more flexible. Instead of having to erase a big part of a paper-based Mind Map or even starting from scratch, you can move things around with a single drag-and-drop motion. I'll discuss the possibilities of computer-based Mind Map software and how they work in Chapter 5.

Benefits of Mind Map

I pointed out several advantages of Mind Map in the previous section where I explained the features. To revisit them, Mind Map allows you to understand a concept faster, more clearly and more thoroughly. Also it provides room for more effective and efficient learning and better recall. It is also very flexible and versatile, as you will see in Chapter 4, where I list various potential uses of Mind Map. You can also approach the concept on a macro as well as micro level. Also, Mind Mapping can be quite fun, once you start experimenting with different colors and symbols.

You don't just have to take my word for it, here are some researches that back up the effectiveness of Mind Map throughout various areas of your mind:

- Memory: Toi (2009) found that Mind Mapping can help children recall words more effectively *(up to 32%)* than using lists.

- Creativity: A study by Al-Jarf (2009) shows that *Mind Mapping software offers a powerful approach for improving the ability of students to generate, visualize and organize ideas.* The students involved reported that the Mind Map encouraged creative thinking and they became faster at generating and organizing ideas for their writing.

- Presentation: Mento et al (1999) reported that executive students using only their Mind Map for presentations were able to *handle challenging questions with confidence.*

- Collaboration in groups: Zampetakis et al (2007) found that students preferred to work with Mind Maps in teams. This allowed them to develop *synergistic interaction, assemble collective knowledge and work with a group minded attitude.*

- Problem solving: Mueller et al (2002) found that the use of Mind Maps in patient care planning at Front Range Community College has resulted in *enhanced thinking skills including critical thinking, whole-brain thinking and comprehensive thinking.*

All in all, **Mind Mapping is a very powerful thinking tool that will enhance the efficiency and effectiveness of how you use your mind.**

Some caveats of Mind Map

When you read about other books on Mind Map such as Tony Buzan's, you might see some excess hype on Mind Mapping. While I love Mind Mapping as a thinking tool, it is not a magic potion that will give you the creativity of Picasso, the analytical genius of Einstein and the memory of the supercomputer chip in an instant, as someone might claim. Let's touch on some of the points so that you have a better understanding on what Mind Map is and what it's not.

Some advocates of Mind Map start from two popular myths that are either scientifically debunked or yet to be proven—the "you only use 10% of your brain" and "left-right brain" myth. They claim that Mind Map is superior because it is a method which balances both sides of your brain rather than only using the analytical left-brain, and because in the process it unlocks the full potential of your brain while normally you only use 10% (or some other variant of that) your brain. I think they are well-meaning and all they are trying to do is promote the benefits of Mind Map. Mind Map really is a wonderful tool and it *works* on many different levels, but the basis of their arguments is myths, not scientific facts. There is even a Wikipedia entry on this, and you can see how the myth is systematically debunked in that article. (Just look up "Ten percent of brain myth" on Wikipedia)

Also, the theory that the left and right hemisphere of the brain has different functionalities and responsibilities (called lateralization theory) is very old and needs some modification. Now scientists believe that, while additional research has to be done, how each hemisphere works is much more complicated than a single clear-cut division across the center of the brain.

What I want to emphasize that while Mind Mapping is not a miracle on Earth, but it still is a powerful tool. Whether or not it is scientifically proven, it passes the most important litmus test for me: practicality. It works in real life, and I've witnessed its effective firsthand in the lives of my own and other people. Also, I think what I've discussed so far in this chapter is sufficient to cover the background on why it is so effective. After all, this is a practical book; and you don't have to know how exactly electricity works in order to reap the benefits of it.

Also, there are people who want to preach that their version of Mind Mapping is the only way the Mind Map should be drawn. They claim that their way is based on the "scientific researches" and it is far superior to others. In my opinion, not only this goes against the very principle which makes Mind Map so powerful—flexibility—but also is not practical. I believe that everyone learns differently, and has a unique combination of visual elements which makes it easier for them to grasp the material. Some might find a colorful, varied Mind Map stimulates their brain and is easier to recall later; the others might find a minimalistic and organized Mind Map works better because there aren't much distraction. Also, a particular style of Mind Mapping will prove effective for one purpose while not suitable for other. Since Mind Map can be used in a wide variety of ways (as you will see in Chapter 4), I believe that there are more than one way to effectively draw a Mind Map with their own benefits.

That said, we will explore various ways that a Mind Map can be drawn in Chapter 3. The whole point is that you can test the different elements and find what works best for you.

Other methods of visual diagramming

In addition to Mind Map, there are several ways to visually represent concepts and ideas. Concept maps and topic maps are popular ones among them. The biggest difference between these methods and Mind Map is that these maps don't have a central key idea and a radial structure; rather, they have several nodes. They are similar to Mind Map in that they also show the relationship between each entry by connecting them with a line. In a nutshell, topic maps can be considered a non-centralized version of Mind Map. Concept maps, on the other hand, is a bit more than that and has some interesting qualities that bear further explanation.

Concept map, as its name suggests, is chiefly used to represent concepts and how they relate to each other. It is first developed by Joseph D. Novak and his research team at Cornell University in the 1970s. While Mind Map only uses one symbol (a line) to denote the connectivity of the concepts, concept map goes further to represent the directionality of that relationship with one- or two-way arrows, and the exact nature of the relationship with annotations. To help you understand, here is an example of concept map on the subject of concept map itself from Wikipedia:

Chapter 1. What Is Mind Map?

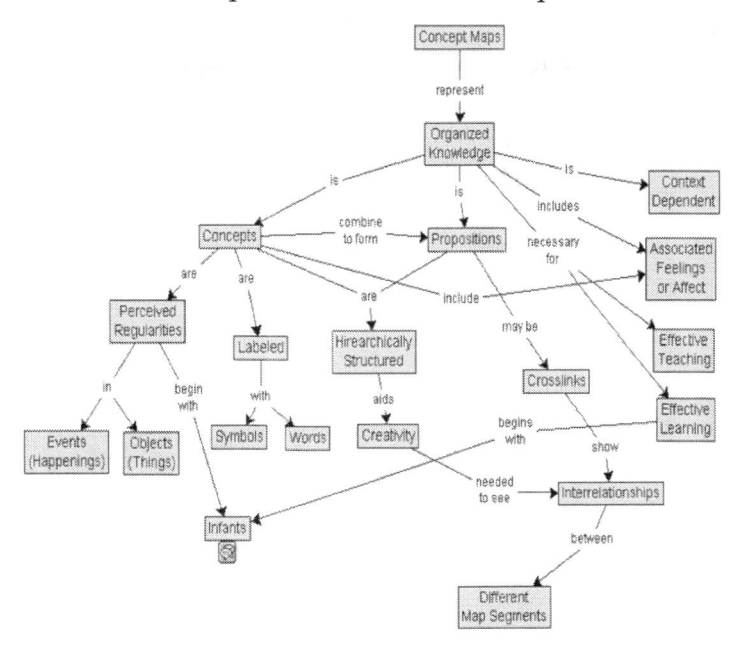

You can notice that while concept maps are decentralized, it has its own starting idea and a hierarchy represented by the vertical alignment (in other words, the concepts progress downward). Also, it relies heavily on language and is verbal in nature, while Mind Map can contain visual representations such as symbols and images. To summarize the comparison between concept maps and Mind Map, concept maps are a specialized visual system for accurately representing the relationship of abstract concepts, while Mind Maps is a more general version that can be used for many other purposes with its unique radial structure.

Chapter 2.
How to Draw A Mind Map

(: the quickest and easiest description you'll ever see)

In the previous chapter, I made a point that at the bare minimum, a Mind Map only needs three elements:

1. Central concept/keyword
2. Sub-concepts/keywords
3. Connecting lines

So, with that in mind, here is the quickest and easiest description you'll ever see of how to draw a Mind Map. Don't be deceived by the simplicity of the technique, you will see diverse the usage of it can be in the following chapters.

First, get a piece of paper. In general the larger the better, but for starters let's make it at least half the size of letter-sized paper. Then, pick a topic, and write it down in the center of the paper.

[My hobbies]

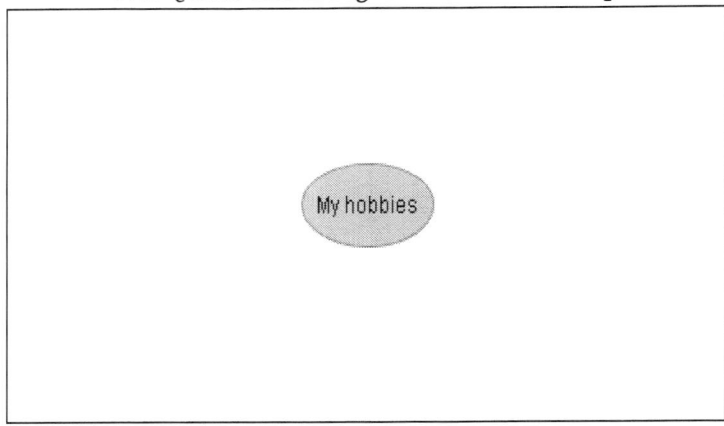

Then, think of things that are directly related to that topic, or the "subcategories" of the topic. Draw a line from the keyword in the center, then write one of the subcategories.

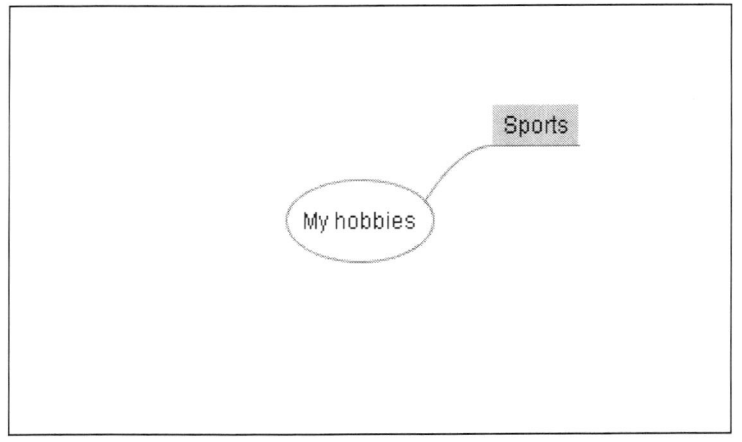

[My hobbies — Sports]

Repeat this step as many times or as little as you like. Generally you will get 3 to 6 subtopics.

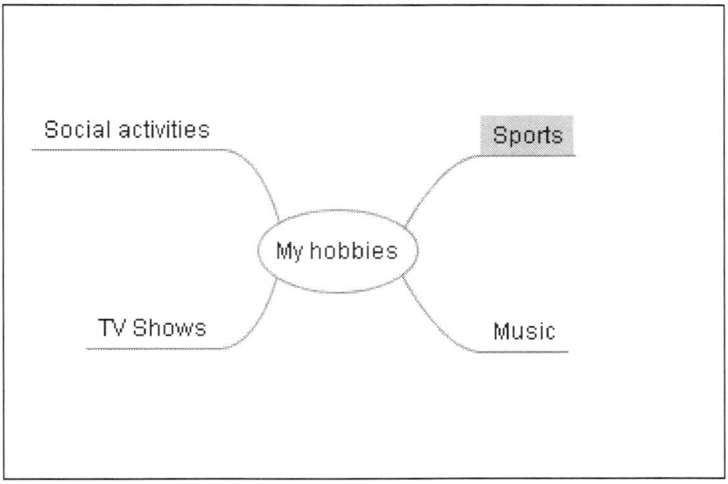
Social activities
Sports
My hobbies
TV Shows
Music

Then, think of subtopics for each subtopic, then repeat the same procedure. You will get something that looks like this:

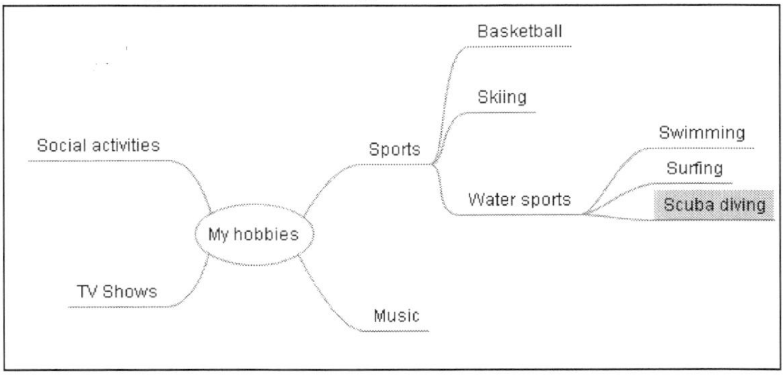
Basketball
Skiing
Swimming
Social activities
Sports
Surfing
Water sports
Scuba diving
My hobbies
TV Shows
Music

Then, you can repeat the steps as many time as you like. In the case of this particular topic, the final product you get might look like this:

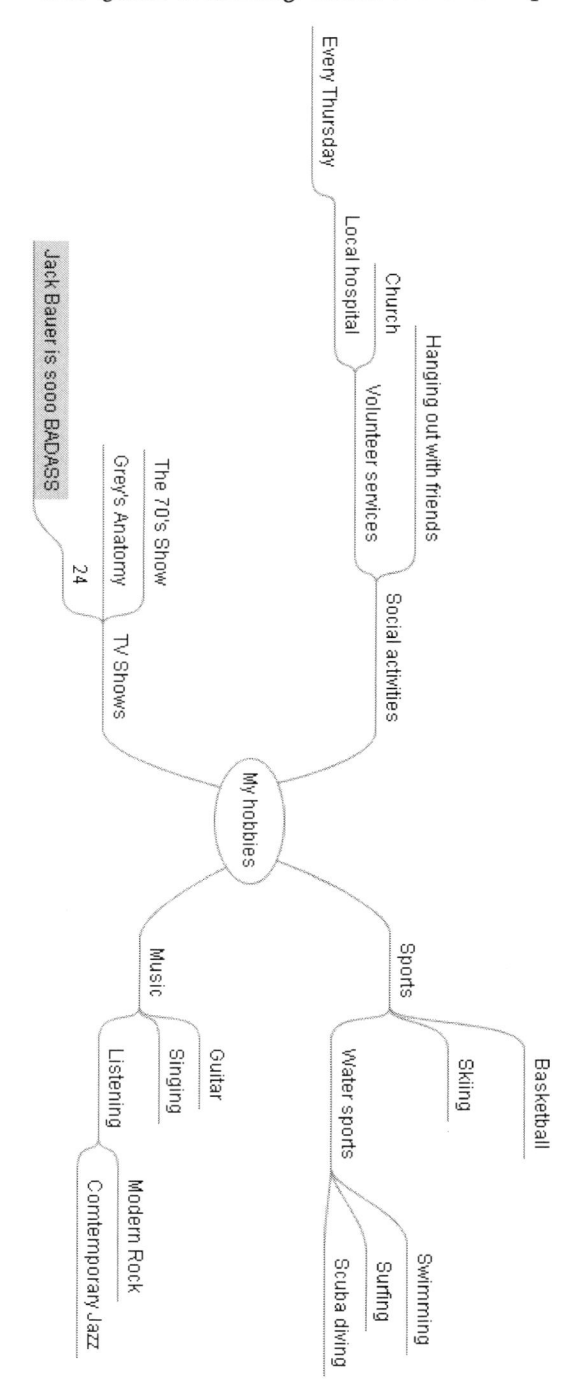

The Quick and Easy Guide to Mind Map

- My hobbies
  - Social activities
    - Hanging out with friends
      - Every Thursday
    - Volunteer services
      - Church
      - Local hospital
  - TV Shows
    - The 70's Show
    - Grey's Anatomy
    - 24 — Jack Bauer is sooo BADASS
  - Sports
    - Basketball
    - Skiing
    - Water sports
      - Swimming
      - Surfing
      - Scuba diving
  - Music
    - Guitar
    - Singing
    - Listening
      - Modern Rock
      - Contemporary Jazz

Chapter 2. How to Draw A Mind Map

That's it. Now you know how to draw a Mind Map, and you are fully equipped to take full advantage of this powerful tool. I encourage you to go ahead and start using this technique in every area of your life, and I'll show you just how to do that in the following chapters.

Chapter 3.
How to Personalize
A Mind Map

While I have only covered the bare minimum in the last chapter, I hope you don't get the impression that there is not much to the technique of Mind Mapping. It's not like that. You can come up with hundreds and thousands of ways to draw a same Mind Map with the same entries, and each version will have a different effect on you. That is why Mind Map can be used for both of two seemingly opposite purposes: creative thinking, which is unrestricted in nature and can be categorized as the so-called "right brain" activity; and organized and analytical thinking, which is more focused and a "left brain" activity [1] Now that you know how to

---

[1] I put them on quotes because as I mentioned earlier, there are no such thing as left-and-right brain tasks. I only used them because I thought it will help your understanding.

draw a Mind Map and hopefully using it in your daily life, let's discuss ways you can experiment with the various elements of Mind Map.

Color

Mind Map is a visual technique, and color is a vital part of your visual senses. While black-and-white Mind Map is much more effective than traditional linear note taking, using colors on a Mind Map opens up a whole new set of possibilities. You can use different colors for each subtopic, or use the colors as a means to highlight particular entries. If there is a pre-established association between a keyword and a color (such as carrot-orange, elephant-gray, or even Democratic party-blue) it can make the connections within your brain that much firmer.

Size

Size is another notable visual element. You can write the keywords that are closer to the central topic bigger to represent the hierarchy, or emphasize a particular word by writing it bigger than other words on the same level. In addition to the words themselves, you can change the thickness of the lines. While some people might find using a uniform weight on all the lines more effective, others

Chapter 3. How to Personalize A Mind Map

might prefer starting out thick, then thinning out as it goes further away from the center, just like the branches do in nature.

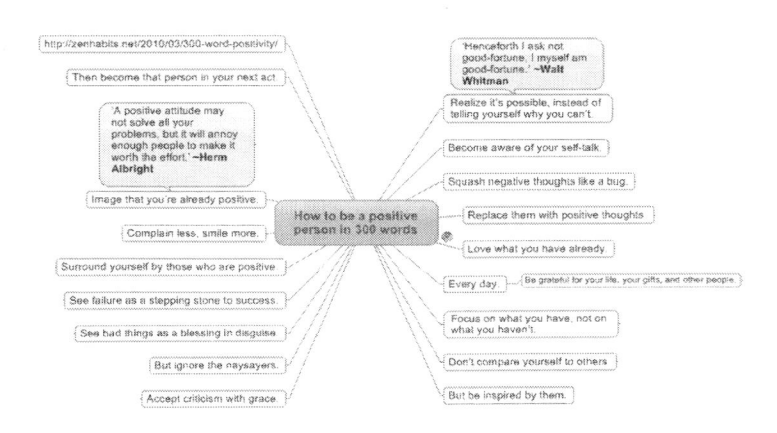

Figure 3-1. Example of Mind Map with fairly uniform keyword size and line weight

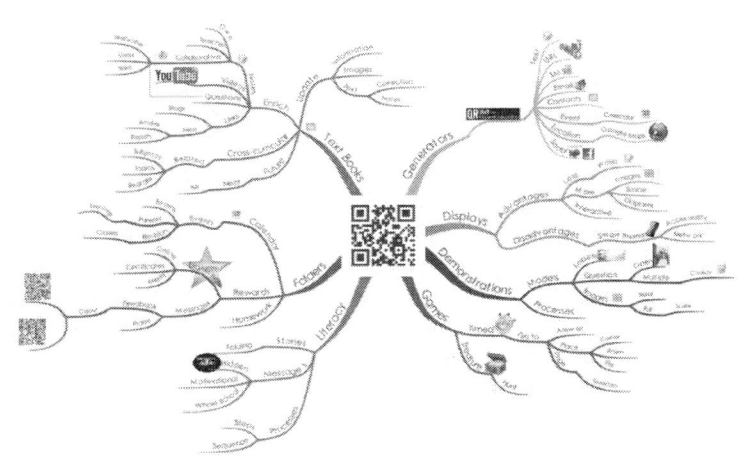

Figure 3-2. Example of Mind Map with varied keyword sizes and weight (Copyright © Alessio Bernardelli)

23

Shapes

You can also use different shapes such as circles, ovals, and rectangles to categorize the concepts or emphasize some over the others. Think about how a flow chart is drawn: it uses different shapes to represent different types of actions (start & finish, action and decision). Shapes are a great way to further organize your thoughts along with color and size.

Lines or shapes?

There are two ways to write the keywords. One is to write them on a line, therefore making the lines continuous as it stems from the central keyword. The other is to write them in a shape or just in an empty space without the lines. Here is an example that shows the two alternatives on one map:

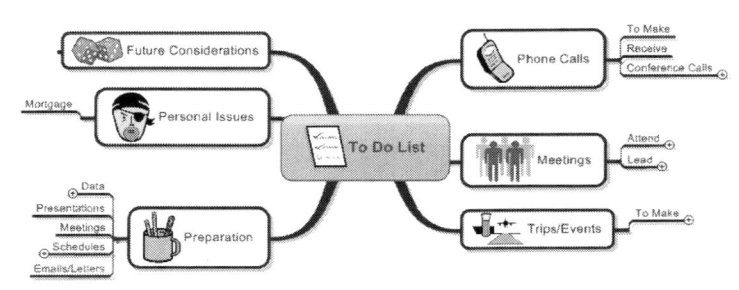

Figure 3-3. Keywords can be written in a shape or on a line.

I think this falls in the category of personal preference. While Tony Buzan claims that keywords should be written on a line, I personally prefer a simple circle, a thin line so that it doesn't interfere the keyword visually, or nothing at all around the keywords. Or you can even use a hybrid form of these two. You can write a keyword in a shape, along with some annotations as necessary above the connecting line, like the concept maps I briefly described in Chapter 1. Whichever way you choose, I advise you to be creative with the process itself and devise new effective ways to organize and represent your thoughts.

Symbol

Here is where the fun begins. Only humans possess the ability to take something as a representation of something else; that is, to use symbols. The words and language used in Mind Maps are a type of symbols too. Since Mind Map triggers your brain to tap into more intuitive functions, symbols are not only a fun twist to your Mind Map but also can be a powerful creativity booster. Start with standard symbols such as the question mark or plus sign, then venture into coming up with your own. If you integrate Mind Map into your everyday life (which I strongly recommend you do), you will find it handy if you can replace some of the recurring concepts or ideas with symbols.

Images

Another fun way to tweak the Mind Map, you can draw or paste an image to represent a concept. If you are doing a hand-drawn Mind Map and you have decent drawing skills, you'll find this enjoyable and visually stimulating for your brain. If you can't draw, don't worry. There are computer-based software programs which provide you with a lot of clip-art samples so you don't have to do it yourself. Chapter 5 will give you a more comprehensive review of computer-based Mind Mapping. Regardless of the method you use, this is a great way to make the Mind Map more "alive" and effective.

Different line shapes

In addition to the thickness that I mentioned earlier, you can experiment with different shapes of the connecting lines. You can make it shorter or longer, straight or curved, the space between them wider or narrower, all depending on the significance of each particular concept or the purpose of your Mind Map. In other words, you might find using straight lines with standard print when organizing a course material for a test, while you might find it more interesting to use curvy lines and funny fonts when you are brainstorming for your short story.

Chapter 3. How to Personalize A Mind Map

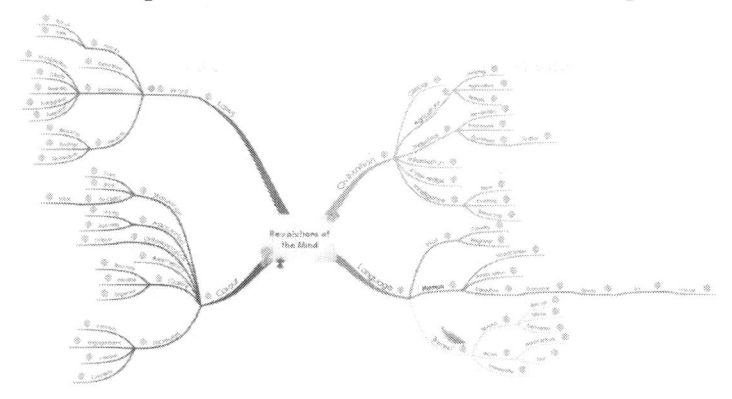

Figure 3-4. Example of free-form Mind Map

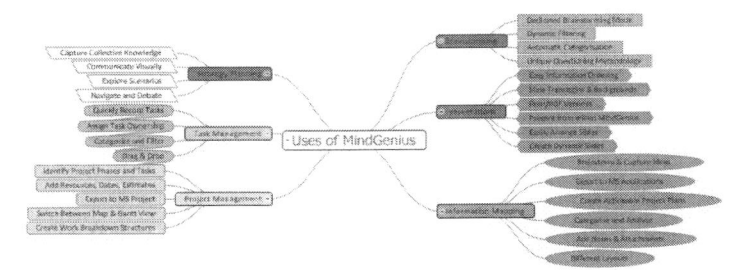

Figure 3-5. Example of "organized" Mind Map

Overall layout of the Mind Map

Combining all the elements (and more, if you can think of other ways) of customization discussed so far, it will be beneficial for you if you can think of the overall layout of the Mind Map and how you will make it fit the purpose for which you are drawing it. As mentioned earlier, if you are trying to organize lecture notes and turn them into a Mind Map which explains the course material thoroughly yet concisely, you might want to make it neat and tidy, with little oddities if any. However, if you are making a presentation and trying to use the Mind Map as a powerful and convincing communication tool, you will want to use some colors along with appropriate symbols and images. Furthermore, in this case, you will experiment with various different arrangements of the ideas in trying to figure out the best and most convincing option; while most of the times you will use the simple chronological order in the case of the lecture notes.

The whole point here is to see what works best for you and what you are trying to achieve. The former is about figuring out the personal propensities and leveraging them to maximize the effectiveness of the Mind Map for you. The latter is about the purpose of the Mind Map and the specific usage of the Mind Map for a specific occasion. The personal preferences you need to do the experimentation yourself. For the purposes, I'll elaborate on them and cover some of the best uses of a Mind Map in the next chapter. As you read along, not only will you notice that the possibilities for Mind Map are almost limitless, but also start to think about what style of Mind Mapping would be best for each use.

Chapter 4.
Potential Uses of Mind Map

In this chapter, I will discuss how you can apply Mind Mapping in your personal and professional life. I tried to be as comprehensive as possible without being too tedious. What I want you to understand after reading this chapter is that Mind Map will improve your efficiency and effectiveness throughout every area of your life. If you are already somewhat familiar to the technique of Mind Mapping, you will find new potential uses in this chapter. Also, for those of you who are using Mind Map in many of these areas and want to take the technique a step further, I have dedicated a chapter (Chapter 6) for that. Meanwhile, let's dive right in.

Brainstorming

One of the most popular and most effective uses of Mind Map is brainstorming. Several features of Mind Map make it an ideal tool for brainstorming. First, Mind Map focuses on one central keyword, so it reduces possible digression and directionless thoughts. Second, Mind Map provides a framework for free association: you can write as many stemming words from a keyword and expand to as many degrees of separation you'd like.

Association is the key to finding new ideas. If you look at the examples of historic invention or scientific breakthrough, you will inevitably notice a pattern where the inventor or scientist got the idea while thinking about something that has some kind of association with the idea. Bill Bowerman got the idea for the "waffle-sole" shoes which launched Nike to be the mega-million giant while having a waffle for breakfast. Also, German Chemist August Kekule was able to figure out the elusive nature of the benzene ring after seeing six snakes forming a circle while holding onto one another's tail in a dream.

Third, the act of writing down the central topic and the ideas around it on a paper has a subtle yet powerful effect on your brain. It gets your brain to generate ideas much better and effectively than you would if you would try to do it all inside your head. You will be able to observe this firsthand if you try to brainstorm in your head and on paper. Finally, the usage of keywords and short key phrases speeds up the process, which is crucial to the brainstorming process. As many of the creative geniuses say in common, the more ideas you get, the higher the chance you'll get a great idea. Therefore it is important that you get as many ideas as you can in as short a timespan as you can. Mind Map is an ideal tool for this; it takes care of both the number and the speed with its principle of association and keyword-orientedness, which I explained in Chapter 1.

When brainstorming with Mind Map, there are several considerations in addition to the speed and number of ideas. In order to let your creative juice to flow, you need to tone down your inner critic for awhile. You might make some spelling errors in the process, or wonder if a particular keyword deserves a place in the Mind Map. In the grand scheme of things, these are insignificant issues. Above all, you need to make sure you get as many ideas as possible. Censoring yourself in the process is only counterproductive. You can sort out these minor errors later, or you might not need them at all!

Use multiple colors and apply a varied style if that helps. You might find the colors and curved lines stimulate your brain and give you some great ideas. Often the process of writing down ideas along with a free association process is enough to get your creative engine going. Once you start using Mind Map for brainstorming, you will see how powerful this simple technique can prove to be.

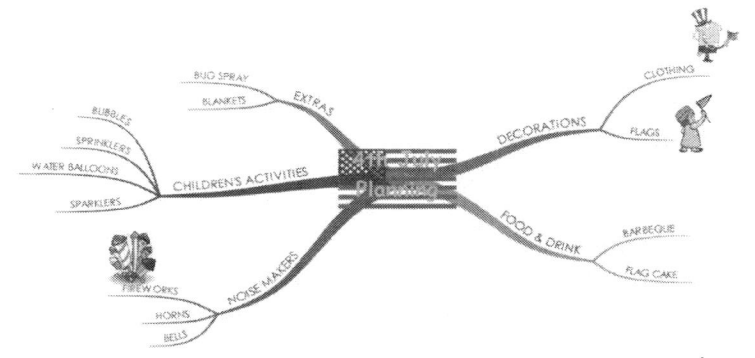

Figure 4-1. Example of Mind Map used for brainstorming on 4th of July plans.

Group brainstorming

As you read along, you will find that Mind Map can be applied on both personal and interpersonal/organizational levels. While you will be the only one who creates and uses the Mind Map when you use it for personal purposes, more than one people can participate in the process of creating and using the Mind Map when used in a group setting. Brainstorming is an excellent example where this comes into play—an area where you can observe the fascinating interplay of different frameworks of thinking.

Group brainstorming can be much more effective than everyone playing solo. This is where the sum of the parts becomes greater than the parts themselves. When people and ideas interact, they give rise to new and improved ideas which have not been

Chapter 4. Potential Uses of Mind Map

accessible before. And Mind Map plays a vital role in this.

When using Mind Map as a group brainstorming tool, there are several ways to do it. First, people can draw their own Mind Maps and share them with the group after they're done. Second, all members of the group can take turns to participate in creating a group Mind Map. Then there are combinations of these two methods; for example, the group can break into subgroups which will bring their Mind Maps to the whole group. Or, individual members can prepare a Mind Map on a subtopic of a subject and be brought together to complete the group Mind Map one cluster at a time.

This method of group brainstorming has several advantages other than the innate effectiveness of Mind Mapping. First, the members can flesh out their ideas fully by expressing them on a Mind Map. Second, along the same line, the participants won't have to worry too much about their ideas being rejected prematurely, because everyone is asked to complete their own Mind Map first or is given equal opportunities to participate in a group Mind Map. Third, by capturing all the ideas on a single Mind Map, the group can make sure that no idea goes unnoticed or gets lost in the process. And last, if executed properly, the process can result in better ideas because all the members are equal participants and can claim ownership of the ideas as a group product. All in all, Mind Map can dramatically increase the effectiveness and the quality of the end-product (the ideas) of group brainstorming.

Creative writing

By the word "creative", I don't mean it in a narrow sense like poetry or fiction writing, while those are certainly part of it. I want to include all kinds of writing where you are writing something new yourself. That includes essays, proposals, reports, theses, and other technical or practical documents. In fact, all of these can be said to be "creative writing", because you are creating something new from scratch.

For many of us, writing something from scratch can be painful. Unless writing is one of your strong suits, you can feel hopeless when you face a blank sheet of paper or your computer screen with a new document open. Mind Map can remove much of this frustration and get you going in writing mode much faster. When you were in high school or college, how did you approach your writing assignment, essay, or theses? We were told to come up with an outline first; however, there are some shortcomings to outlining.

First, when outlining, many people feel they need to come up with something neat and tidy while we can't have a full grasp of the subject on the first attempt. Therefore we often feel discouraged when certain blind spots or "fuzzy areas" come up while outlining. Second, by trying to think chronologically from the beginning to an end, we put a limit on our creativity. The ideas don't come necessarily in a linear order. Rather almost always the ideas come randomly at first, then you arrange it in an order which makes the most sense. Trying to flesh out an outline first restrains the brainstorming function of your brain because you are going against the natural tendency of the brain.

Now don't get me wrong; I am not trying to say that outlining is useless and you need to throw out outlining altogether. My point is that while an outline is an essential part for a coherent and organized writing product, you can't come up with a good outline by tackling the outline first.

What's the alternative? Well, in order to address the shortcomings addressed earlier, it is clear that you need to have a process of pouring out ideas so that you need something to work with, the "basic ingredients" for outlining. Here is where Mind Map comes in. Mind Mapping can help you not only in brainstorming for the content, but organizing them into a meaningful outline as well. In fact, you can create an outline in the form of a Mind Map, rather than traditional list-form outline. First, you want to write everything you know about or have done research on a subject down on a piece of paper, and Mind Map is a perfect way to do this. Once you can see all the information and bits of ideas on a piece of paper, you can start to organize the ideas in a meaningful way. You can choose what to write on and what to leave out, then move the ideas around until it makes a coherent outline.

So next time you need to write something, use the guidelines I've just presented and see how much more quickly and effectively you brainstorm and more coherent and convincing your outline becomes. In fact, this is how precisely I wrote this book. I've done a full-on brainstorming on the subject of Mind Map, then organized the topics into a draft Mind Map that looked like this:

Chapter 4. Potential Uses of Mind Map

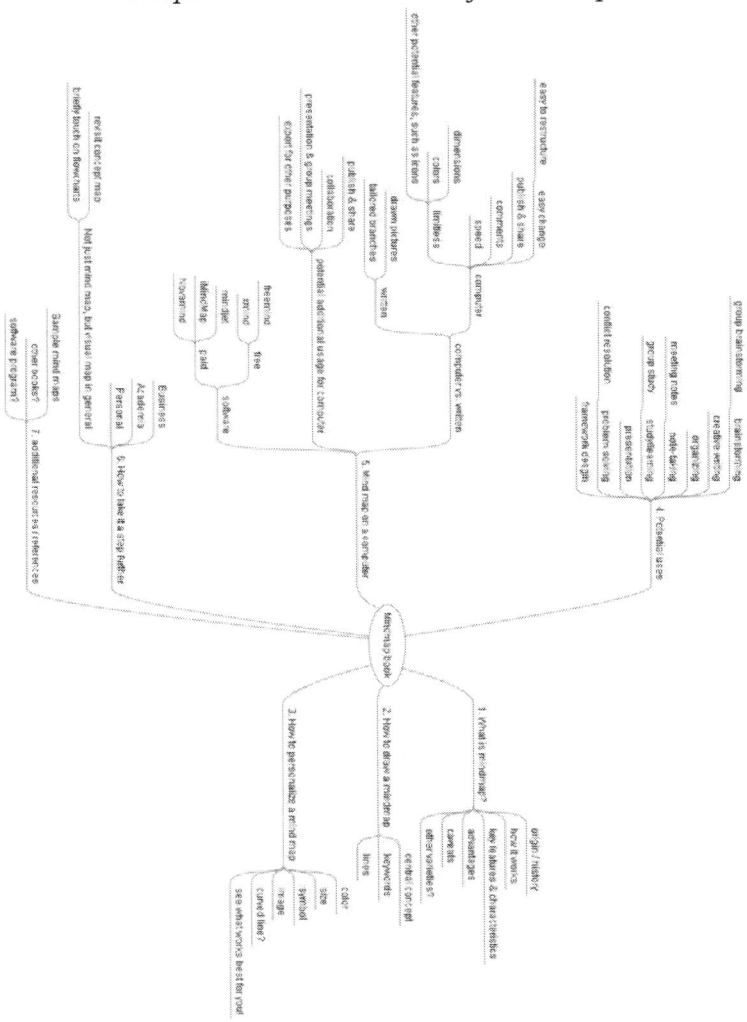

Figure 4-2. Mind Map used for planning and outlining this book.

Now I have to confess, I haven't been the best writer in the world when I was in grade school. However, ever since I've used this technique, I've found writing much easier and enjoyable than before. One of the challenges I had in the past was to figure out what I would write on. Now, with the help of

37

Mind Map, I can come up with a full outline in less than thirty minutes!

Organizing information

Earlier in the book I've briefly mentioned that Mind Map can serve both the creative side and the analytical side of your brain. So far we discussed how Mind Map can be used to cater the creative side. Yet, Mind Map can be equally effective in the analytical usage. Let me start with one of the most common examples, which is organizing information.

In the previous paragraphs explaining how you can use Mind Map for creative writing, I have touched on how you can first brainstorm then organize the ideas, all using Mind Map. In fact, Mind Map can be used to organize just about anything. What makes Mind Map great for this purpose is the focus on a central keyword and the clustering which enables you both the snapshot view and detailed information.

You can organize course materials, professional information, systems and processes, to-do lists, or even shopping lists. You can try Mind Mapping wherever you feel overloaded with information or need more clarity. As you get good at it, you will be able to create your own "cheat sheet" of whatever information you need to better understand and handle. Not just take my word for it; I

Chapter 4. Potential Uses of Mind Map

want you to try it for yourself. When you have time, create a Mind Map of what you've learned in your chemistry class, the various elements of your next project, or the options for your next family vacation plan including the different interests of your family members. You will be amazed at how clearer your thinking seems to become, and how the information which seemed so overwhelming feels more manageable.

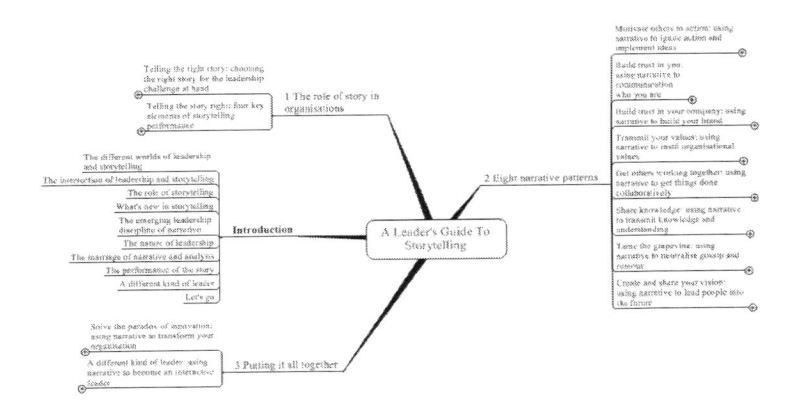

Figure 4-3. A sample Mind Map used for book summary.

Note taking

This use and the next several ones can be classified into the broad category of organizing information. If you are a student, Mind Map can give you an unfair advantage over others because this powerful tool hasn't gone mainstream yet among students.

Students often fall prey to one of the two extremes of note taking. They write either too little so they have trouble with recollection, or too much so they don't have any room left to really take in the lecture and process the information. The point of note taking is not to reproduce the entire lecture later. It is supposed to act as a supplement in your studying. Therefore, as a general rule, you need to find a medium ground between the two extremes.

Not all the materials in a lecture are created equal. Some are key points which are crucial for your understanding of the subject matter, while others are "just-so-you-know" information. In order to effectively identify what matters and what doesn't, you need to be able to grasp the big picture at all times during a lecture. Here is where Mind Map comes in. While some people suggest that you only take notes in a Mind Map format, I don't suggest you do so when you are starting out. Identifying what matters is a skill which takes some time to master. Until you become more adept in separating the wheat from the chaff, I suggest you use Mind Map as an accompanying device to your main note-taking method.

Here's how you do it. Get a separate sheet of paper besides your notebook, and write down the name of the class or the subject of that particular lecture in the center. Then, as the lecture proceeds, try to follow along by using keywords and key concepts as the basis of your Mind Map note. Let the details be handled by your textbook or your main notebook. The purpose here is to draw a big picture, and get used to classifying and processing information as they are presented real-time.

As you use this method of note-taking more frequently, you'll notice that your thinking and comprehension improves. You'll be more efficient in your studying, because you will be able to better understand how the key concepts relate to each other. In the end, you will be getting better grades while studying less. It is all about efficiency and effectiveness, not just hard work. And Mind Map is a great tool which enhances both efficiency and effectiveness in anything that has to do with your mind.

Meeting notes

Note taking is not confined in the classroom setting. One of the examples where Mind Map can be useful for note taking outside of academia is meeting notes in a corporate environment. You can use Mind Map in real-time as I have explained earlier, or as an organizing tool after the meeting, depending on the propensity of the user or appropriateness for the occasion. When using Mind Map for this purpose, there are several tips that will increase the effectiveness of the Mind Map. First, try using different shapes or colors for each participant and different symbols for the nature of a comment—a proposition, a question, a request for follow-up, etc. When doing this, try to make a category for items that are actionable or require further action. You can even collect everything of this nature and list them as a subtopic of the Mind Map.

With the advent of computer-based Mind Map software, the possibility for using Mind Map for meeting notes has increased exponentially(In the next chapter I will explain more on how computer enhances the functions of Mind Map). You can easily share a Mind Map with all the participants who can make revisions and clarifications on what they have said or meant. Then, the revised Mind Map can act as an action plan which can keep all of the members engaged. The advantage of Mind Map over traditional methods of group communication comes from the increased clarity Mind Map is able to provide; everyone can understand the whole landscape more clearly, and this is more conducive to positive action and problem-solving.

Chapter 4. Potential Uses of Mind Map

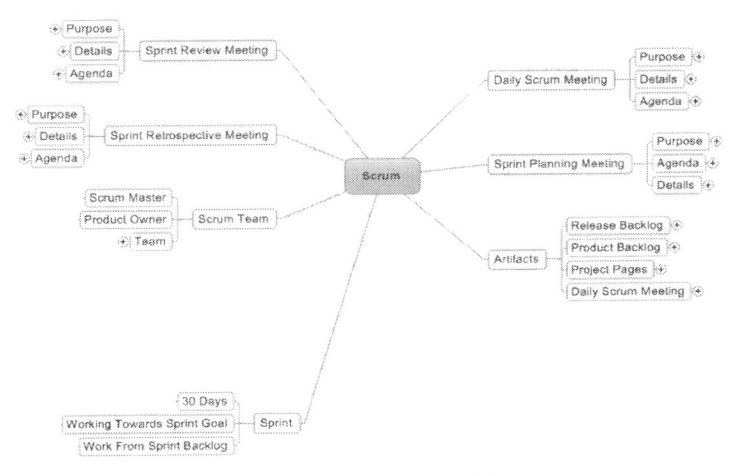

Figure 4-4. Example of a "rough draft" meeting notes

Study/learning

Mind Map is simply a great tool for studying and learning. In fact, author and college professor Toni Krasnic wrote a great book on this subject, How to Study with Mind Maps. He uses visual mapping (which includes but is not limited to Mind Map) as the cornerstone of his learning method, CLM (Concise Learning Method). Although the primary audience in his book is students, this book is a great resource for anyone who is serious about learning. Here's a Mind Map by Professor Krasnic on the advantage that Mind Map brings to students:

The Quick and Easy Guide to Mind Map

Figure 4-5. Top 10 Mind Mapping uses for students (Copyright © Toni Krasnic)

Group Study

If you are involved in a group study environment, Mind Map can be used to improve the effectiveness of learning dramatically. Everyone has a different understanding of a subject matter, and blind spots can arise if one only considers her version of understanding. Mind Map provides a framework where everyone can communicate and contribute their take on a subject matter to the whole group. As I have mentioned earlier while explaining how to use Mind Map for group brainstorming, you can use Mind Mapping in a group study in one of three ways: individuals complete their own Mind Map then bring those together; everyone participates in creating a group Mind Map; or a combination of the two. If the subject matter is more analytical and clear-cut, such as mathematics or chemistry, the group making a single Mind Map together can be more suitable. If the subject warrants more discussion and exchange of opinions such as literature and philosophy, the group members can find it more effective to lead the discussion based on the Mind Maps they created on their own. Whichever method a group uses, including Mind Map as a tools for organizing and communicating information will help the understanding and retention of the material for the participants, as well as discovery of new and creative ideas.

Presentation

Mind Map is becoming increasingly popular as a tool for presentation. As I have explained earlier on how to create an outline with a Mind Map, it can be used as a means to creating the material and preparing for a presentation. Not only that, but Mind Map itself can be used as the presentation material. People are discovering the benefits of using Mind Map in a presentation because it can present ideas in a more clear, concise and compelling manner. In a more informal setting, some people even choose to use a single Mind Map broken into clusters as the presentation slides. This cuts the time and extra work in preparing a slide from an outline, but you might find this appropriate or not depending on your particular situation. There are several points you need to consider in using Mind Map as a part of a presentation:

- Make sure the Mind Map has a purpose and something it's trying to communicate. If it doesn't pass the "so what?" test, it is nothing more than a pretty graphic.
- Make the Mind Map visually compelling and easy to understand.
- Use multiple colors and symbols when appropriate.
- Consider what layout of the Mind Map has the most impact on the viewer.

Chapter 4. Potential Uses of Mind Map

Problem solving

Problem solving requires a high level of intellectual and cognitive coordination. It requires you to clearly define what the problem is, come up with the possible solutions or alternatives, evaluate the validity and associated risk for each, and then decide on what action to take. Because it requires your mind to be engaged on some serious thinking, Mind Map can surely be of help, just like any other act that involves your mind.

Mind Map can be used in any of the four stages of problem solving that I have just mentioned, namely;

- Defining the problem
- Brainstorming possible solutions
- Evaluate the solutions
- Decision-making

First off, you might start with writing everything you can think about the problem on a Mind Map. Sometimes problem solving is made hard because one does not know exactly what the problem is, or thinks that the problem is something other than it really is. Clearing your head and writing everything down on a piece of paper and organizing the thoughts in a meaningful structure can help you see the problem clearly as well as start thinking about the possible solutions.

When you have a Mind Map of the problem itself, you may or may not create a separate Mind Map to brainstorm some possible solutions. Often you'll get hints of the solutions from the first Mind Map you have created. Then, you can evaluate the solutions on a Mind Map. Here are some points of reference which will help your thinking; the 5W1H (who, when, where, what, why and how), "what if"'s, risks, advantages and disadvantages, the feasibility of the solution, and so on.

Then, you can review all the Mind Maps you have made in the process to make the decision. Not only will the Mind Maps speed up the steps in the process, but also provide a framework for more comprehensive information and reference for you to make a better decision.

Conflict resolution

Conflict resolution is where the problem solving process I have just described is brought to an interpersonal dimension. Problem solving, as I have used the term in the above paragraphs, is a process where an individual or a group is trying to deal with a problem internally; whereas conflict resolution indicates that the problem involves two or more entities. In other words, it is problem solving between two or more individuals or organizations.

Mind Map can prove to be useful when each entity tries to communicate where they are coming from to the other side. Just as one would do in a problem solving situation, you can map out the problem as you understand

Chapter 4. Potential Uses of Mind Map

it. This will help the other side understand the situation on your side, and how you really view the problem. Most conflict arises from the difference in the background and interpretation of a situation. Through Mind Map, you can more clearly communicate your position to the other side. You don't have to bring the Mind Map to the other side and explain each keyword, though it will be very effective; just doing the work yourself will bring more clarity to your own understanding of the situation and make you more effective in communicating it to the other side. If the other side is familiar with the technique of Mind Map, great! You can suggest to the other side that each of you do a Mind Map on the problem and bring it together. It will definitely uncover some hidden issues and hot buttons which otherwise would have left unnoticed. Try this in your personal and professional relationship; you will find yourself become a much more effective communicator and negotiator.

Systematic design

Mind Map is an excellent way to design and portray systems and processes. Mind Map is gaining more popularity in the corporate world, and it is recognized as an important visual tool along with flow charts. In developing a process, you need to figure out all the essential aspects that constitutes that

The Quick and Easy Guide to Mind Map

process. You need to know the purpose, the desired outcome, the available resources, and so on. This is where the creative side of Mind Map comes into play. You can address all these issues and make sure you are ready to design a process.

Also, Mind Map can be the end product, a tool for describing the completed system and process. In fact, when used in conjunction with flow charts, Mind Map can be one of the best tools to graphically represent a system, as you can see in the example below.

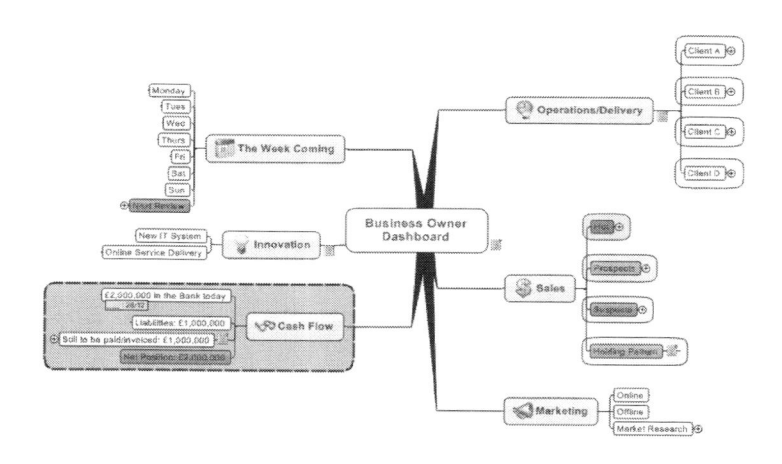

Figure 4-6. Example of a business owner's management system outlined by a Mind Map (Copyright © Liam Hughes)

So far we have discussed some of the potential uses you can apply Mind Map to. I hope that you are now seeing how vast the possibilities with Mind Map can be, and I have barely scratched the surface here. As I have said many times, Mind Map will increase the

Chapter 4. Potential Uses of Mind Map
efficiency and effectiveness of anything you do with your mind. Regardless of your familiarity with the technique, you will find more ways you can use the Mind Map. I hope after reading this book you are starting to reap the benefits of this wonderful thinking tool.

Chapter 5.
Mind Map on A Computer

Since Tony Buzan has popularized Mind Mapping in the 1970s, there has been a fundamental shift in how one can use this technique in recent years with the arrival of computer and internet, then Web 2.0 and mobile smart devices. This has opened up a whole new set of possibilities for what's already a vastly powerful tool, and I haven't seen many books allowing for the discussion of this issue as it deserves. In this chapter, I am going to address how the computer and smart devices along with the instant connectivity of the internet has brought a massive change in how you can use Mind Map. I will show you some advantages computerized Mind Map has over hand-written Mind Map, and I'll briefly introduce some of the Mind Mapping software.

Computerized vs. hand-written Mind Map

There are several features a Mind Map software program has that a traditional hand-written Mind Map doesn't have which include: ease of modification, speed, long text entry, maneuverability, connectivity and limitlessness. Let me address them one by one.

a. Ease of modification

Obviously, this is one of the characteristics of any digital form. If you are old enough to know how a typewriter works, compare it to the word processing software we have now. That's the difference between a computerized and hand-written Mind Map. You don't need an eraser to correct a misspelling or change a keyword on Mind Map software; you literally perform those functions at your fingertips. Also, you can rearrange the whole Mind Map and move around the clusters and keywords with some clicks and drag-and-drops, while you have to start from scratch and draw the whole Mind Map again with a hand-drawn Mind Map.

b. Speed

In line with the last feature, Mind Map software enables you to create a Mind Map relatively faster than the hand-written option. Many people find that typing is faster than handwriting for them, which means people can draw the same Mind Map faster on a

Chapter 5. Mind Map on A Computer

computer. Also, there is no need to draw the lines when using Mind Map software; few strokes of keys and you can insert as many subkeywords to a keyword, which makes it not only faster but easier.

c. Long text entry

Sometimes when you are creating a Mind Map, there are times that you want to include some written detail relevant to the subject. However, traditional hand-written Mind Map does not provide much room to accommodate that. With most of the Mind Map software out there today you can add a "note" to a particular keyword. Also, computerized Mind Map makes it much easier to incorporate long sentences into the Mind Map, because typed characters remain neat and legible. If you are trying to achieve that, it is not likely to happen unless you have a very neat handwriting.

d. Maneuverability

By maneuverability, I mean that there are several functionalities in a typical Mind Mapping program which is only made possible on a computer. For example, you can zoom in and out of a Mind Map, change fonts, change font sizes, "fold" and "expand" nodes, merge multiple Mind Maps, export a cluster of a Mind Map to make it another stand-alone Mind Map, and many others. These are only just a starting point, because what computers can do with Mind Maps really starts to become much more interesting when the internet and networking comes in, as I'll address in the next feature.

e. Connectivity

Many high-end Mind Map software programs enable you to share your Mind Map with others. It can be that your colleagues at work can modify the meeting notes you wrote; however, there is much more to that. You can publish your Mind Map into a pdf file, a document file, an image file, or even to a webpage. The published Mind Map on a webpage doesn't have to be a static one; you can let people manipulate the Mind Map in the ways I have just mentioned above by embedding your Mind Map as an application! (If you don't understand what I am talking about, think about a blog post with a Youtube video in it. It's not just a "dead" object, when you click the play button, the video comes live. It is like that).

Also, as mobile devices such as smartphones and tablet PCs have gained more popularity recently, the software developers released mobile version of their software. Now you can review and modify the Mind Maps you made on your computer on your Android phone or your iPad, which means, at the very least, you have this powerful thinking tool at your disposal virtually anywhere you go, anytime.

There is so much more you can do with the use of Mind Map software with the mobile and Web 2.0 technology, I feel like I'm almost limiting the concept by categorizing all of them under a single term "connectivity." Maybe that can be compensated by the last characteristic which is named:

    f. Limitlessness

If you are creating a hand-drawn Mind Map, the paper you use can be only so large. If you go beyond a certain point, it becomes impractical and unfeasible. However, there is no limit to the dimension of your computerized Mind Map. Not only that, you can use as much colors as you'd like (of course, until you have used so many that you cannot tell one from the other), and as many sub-keywords as you'd like under a keywords. Also, many software programs include hundreds if not thousands of icons, images and clip-arts that you can use anywhere appropriate. Last but not least, most of the programs provide you with diverse templates, polygons and line shapes, bringing the customization discussed in Chapter 3 to your fingertips. In summary, you can practically create a limitless number of Mind Maps of limitless dimensions in limitless number of variations. If this doesn't qualify for unleashing a huge potential for organizing and representing information and your thinking, I don't know what does.

Should I desert hand-drawn Mind Map altogether?

While the difference between computer-based and hand-drawn Mind Maps is like that of a typewriter and a word-processor, I personally think that hand-drawn Mind Maps still has its place. After all, the good ol' pen and paper didn't go extinct even though our primary method of writing switched to computers. Also, some people still deliberately choose to write with a pen instead of a keyboard, and when the person's mastery with her pen exceeds a certain level it becomes an art form called calligraphy

However, unlike calligraphy, hand-drawn Mind Maps do have practical uses. Creative Mind Map is a great example. For artistically inclined people, the Mind Map software, however awesome they might be, can come short in representing those people's thoughts and ideas. Think about the occasions you ever heard a painter deserting his watercolors in favor of Photoshop. There are certain areas that technology can never replace a human being, and one such area is creativity. Hand-drawn Mind Maps, although it might be less convenient, is the ultimate customization method.

Rather than me explaining it further, let me give you an excellent example of a creative hand-drawn Mind Map from Buzan Centre Australia:

Chapter 5. Mind Map on A Computer

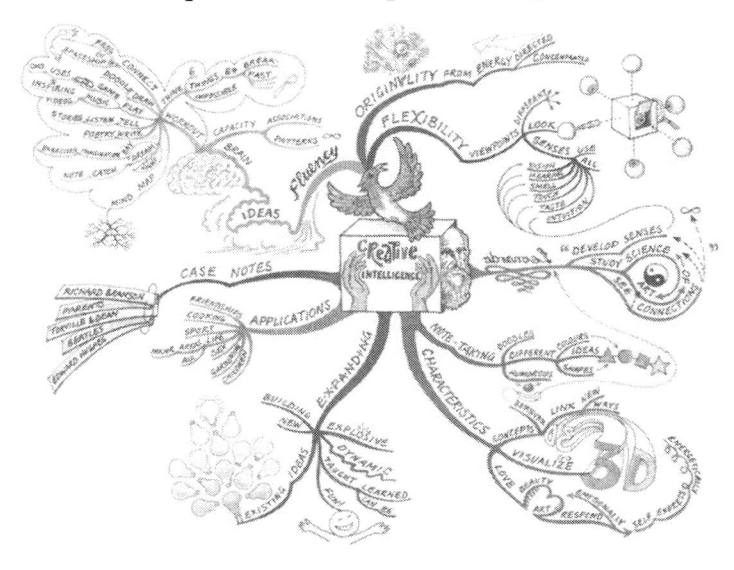

If you ask me if there is any software that is capable of reproducing such artistically pleasing, visually compelling and creatively stimulating Mind Map, I would have to say I haven't seen one yet nor I think I will see one in the near future.

Another instance where hand-drawn Mind Map can be useful is when you need to quickly jot down ideas. I still carry a pen and paper with me wherever I go even though I can use my iPhone to make notes or even voice recordings, because the usefulness of pen and paper is still relevant after all the technological advance. The back of a receipt at the right time can be much more powerful than the Mind Mapping program with the latest upgrades later.

Having given the hand-written Mind Map its fair share of defense, let's move on to how you can use your computer-based Mind Map.

Potential usages for computer-based Mind Map

I have briefly touched upon these usages briefly when I was explaining the advantages computer-based Mind Map have; however, let's dig a bit deeper because they are worth exploring.

a. Publishing & sharing

The internet has made it really easy and simple to publish your Mind Map and share it with your friends, classmates and colleagues. In a professional environment, you can send a project outline in a Mind Map form to your supervisor before sending her a full project plan. Not only will it be easier for her to understand but also a huge time-saver. In a more personal setting, you can send a Mind Map you have done on a book you have recently read as an attachment in an email recommending the book to your friend.

As if internet wasn't enough, the advent of mobile devices and cloud computing took publishing and sharing to a whole new level. Now you can draw a Mind Map, view other Mind Maps you have created at home and uploaded to your personal cloud storage, publish them to your blog, and share them with your friends instantly, anywhere you are

Chapter 5. Mind Map on A Computer

(as long as you have wireless internet connection), with your smartphone! As one of the primary function of Mind Map is more efficient and effective organization and presentation of ideas, this publishing and sharing technology allows you to facilitate sharing of meaningful information and gives you a chance to contribute to the advancement of humanity. Now that might sound far-fetched, yet that is essentially what you are doing once you get serious about fully utilizing Mind Map in every area of your life.

   b. Collaboration

     While hand-written Mind Map can be created by more than one person, it is limited by the boundaries of time and space. In other words, the participants have to be in the same location at the same time, otherwise it would take a very long time to create one. However, the instant connectivity provided by the internet renders this requirement unnecessary. Now people can participate in creating a Mind Map while sitting at their home or office. Although it might not be as effective as figuring things out face-to-face, it can be compensated by the sheer ease and ubiquity of the communication. When two or more people at a distance are discussing a complex subject such as a new business venture or their new artistic collaboration, Mind Map can be a crucial tool in clearly communicating what one participant is thinking to the others.

c. Presentation & group meetings

While hand-drawn Mind Maps can be used for these purposes, computerized Mind Map makes it so much easier. When was the last time you saw cellophane films used as a means of presentation? Because the primary tool for presentation has shifted to computer programs, computerized Mind Maps are much more relevant than hand-drawn ones. Also, the ease of change and the limitlessness of computer-based Mind Maps make it suitable for taking notes or creating a framework in a group setting.

d. Repurpose

As I have mentioned earlier, you can use the "export" function of the Mind Map software to convert the Mind Map into other forms. The most common form would be an image file. While the image cannot be modified, it is the easiest format to use for most purposes, such as email attachment, part of a document, etc. Also, you can turn a part of a Mind Map into a separate Mind Map. An example of this usage would be breaking down a complex and comprehensive master map of a project into bite-sized Mind Maps for easier understanding (e.g. each phase as a center keyword for each Mind Map).

Just as I have pointed out in earlier chapters, Mind Map has many uses and you can repurpose Mind Map in as many ways. Computer-based Mind Map makes this much

Chapter 5. Mind Map on A Computer

easier because you can keep the original intact and create original or modified copies without using too much resource such as time and money.

A list of Mind Map software

After reading all the good things about Mind Map software, you might be eager to get started right away and plunge into the world of digital Mind Mapping. Here is a list of free and paid Mind Mapping software. Each come with different features and advantages, yet unless you are an advanced Mind Mapper the free ones have all the necessary features for you to get going. So I suggest you start with one of the free options, get used to it, then venture into paid ones if you feel like. I personally like Freemind because it is free and simple. Among the paid ones, MindMeister, Novamind and Xmind are among the good ones.

Free Mind Mapping Software
- Freemind
- Freeplane
- SciPlore Mind Mapping
- XMIND

Paid Mind Mapping Software
- 3D Topicscape
- Buzan's iMind Map
- Creately
- Inspiration

- LucidChart
- Microsoft Visio
- Mind42
- MindGenius
- MindManager
- MindMapper
- MindMeister
- MindView
- NovaMind
- PersonalBrain
- Qiqqa
- SmartDraw
- SpicyNodes
- Visual Mind
- XMind Pro

For more information on the specific features of each software, refer to the table in the Appendix.

Chapter 6.
How to Take It
A Step Further

Up to this point, I have given you the complete package—what Mind Map is, how to draw one, how you can use it, and how you can take advantage of the existing technology for more possibilities. If you are new to Mind Map, I urge you start using Mind Map to get your feet wet as soon as possible. The most amazing tool in the world wouldn't mean anything if you don't use it. I really hope that this book works as a catalyst in bringing positive change in your life, and the technique I shared with you in here can bring that kind of result. Start with small things—jotting down your thoughts, sorting out your grocery list, figuring out what you want to do for your next vacation. Once you see the benefits firsthand, using the tools will become easier and more natural for you.

If you were already familiar with the technique before you picked up this book, here's my suggestion for you. You were probably looking for more ideas for where to apply the tool, or more advanced tactics in using Mind Map. I suggest you go to Chapter 4 and review it thoroughly. I have given you lots of ideas about the potential uses of Mind Map. In my opinion, the difference between an advanced Mind Map user and someone who is just starting out is not in the slick and ninja tactics the former only possesses(I don't even know if there's such a thing), but in how more broadly she applies the technique across different areas of her life than the latter does. The broader and more frequent your use of Mind Map is, the more adept you will become in using the tool and the more ideas you will get for where to use the tool. As you review Chapter 4, I am sure you will get lots of ideas for new ways you can use Mind Map.

Of course, as you get more experienced with using Mind Map, you will develop your own tips and techniques. However, as I have mentioned earlier, I believe that Mind Map is highly customizable in nature. In other words, what works for someone might not be so effective for another. Moreover, the Mind Map software programs are equipped with so many advanced features that anyone has access to incorporating different elements into their own Mind Map. You have all these tools at your disposal; yet they won't mean much unless you can use them in a way that is meaningful

Chapter 6. How to Take It A Step Further

to you. I think that comes from experience in drawing your own maps and observing how others do it.

I have already addressed how you can get more experience on your own by broadening the scope of which you use Mind Map in your life. In terms of observing how others do it, there is a great resource online where you can view thousands of Mind Maps on tens of different subjects. It is called Biggerplate (www.biggerplate.com). It's an online Mind Map library where users can upload their own Mind Map. Not only you can observe some "best practices" there, you can download and use the Mind Maps for yourself. There are some good ones—I found the business analyses and book summaries very useful.

So far I have focused the discussion of how to take Mind Mapping a step further on the personal domain. There are two more important areas worth mentioning; academic and business uses. Since Mind Map is a tool for processing information and presenting it in a way that's more conducive for comprehension, I think it should be the core tool for anyone who is serious about learning. Learning is a process of understanding, internalizing and applying information. Mind Map can be very powerful in each of these steps, especially the first two. I personally think that any course material should be organized using Mind Map (not to be dogmatic, but simply because it is effective!). It's even proved experimentally (cited from an article from Tony Buzan's ThinkBuzan.com):

- Goodnough and Woods (2002) discovered that students perceived Mind Mapping as a fun, interesting and motivating approach to learning. Several students attributed the fun aspect to the opportunity to be creative when creating Mind Maps through lots of choice in color, symbols, key words and design.

- Mind Mapping has been shown to bring a renewed sense of enthusiasm to the classroom because it increases student confidence and sense of skill in mastering assigned materials (Mento et al, 1999).

- Using Mind Mapping software in the classroom is a successful way to support children's exploration and presentation of ideas. Ralston and Cook (2007) found that an exercise involving Mind Mapping software provided a useful focus for pupils to organize their thoughts and to present information clearly and attractively. It also facilitated communication between pupils.

By summarizing the material in a Mind Map form, you will notice that you get a better and clearer understanding of it. Professor Toni Krasnic, who I have mentioned earlier, has formulated a learning method based on visual maps (of which Mind Map is a central part), called Concise Learning Method (CLM). I found it very effective, so if you want to learn

Chapter 6. How to Take It A Step Further

how to apply Mind Map to your learning, check his book out. His book presents a complete model and thoroughly covers all the aspects and is fun to read, with well-placed quotes and cartoon strips.

When you visit Biggerplate, you will notice that Mind Map is already being widely used in business settings. If you haven't personally observed it being used in your company or organization, you can make a valuable contribution by being the first to introduce this tool. Profit-driven corporations are all about efficiency and effectiveness, and if they're adopting a tool widely, I think that's telling something. As I have discussed in Chapter 4, Mind Map can be very powerful in fostering professional efficiency and effectiveness for individuals and groups. Mind Maps are not just a fancy artwork with colors and shapes—it can bring meaningful changes in systematic and analytical thinking. So, when you spot an opportunity to bring up and introduce this technique to your team or coworkers, such as brainstorming for a new product idea or developing a complex project, don't hesitate! Often times people can notice the benefits of Mind Map as soon as they observe the power of a well-drawn Mind Map brings, and it will take no time before Mind Map becomes the engine that drives the thinking of your organization.

In Closing...

I hope you have enjoyed reading this book, and are already busy implementing Mind Map in every area of your life and experiencing the benefits. I truly believe in its power to transform your personal and professional effectiveness, so I will be very glad if the knowledge I've shared with you found a good use.

If you have enjoyed this book, I will greatly appreciate if you can leave me an honest review on Amazon (you can go to ImproveYourMemoryToday.net/review_MM and you will be taken to the review page directly) or tell your friends about this book. That way, I can make sure that you are doing great with the information shared in this book, and that others can benefit from this book too.

Meanwhile, if you want something to complement what you have learned so far and take your mental capacity to the next level, you can check out my other books:

The Quick and Easy Guide to Memory Improvement: 45 Practical Tips You Can Use to Boost Your Memory
(details: improveyourmemorytoday.net/book)

The Quick and Easy Guide to Mnemonics: Improve Your Memory Instantly with 15 Powerful Memory Aids
(details: improveyourmemorytoday.net/book2)

Chapter 6. How to Take It A Step Further

These books give you a detailed explanation on how you can improve your memory and recall through the power of practical tips and exercises, and a powerful memory tool called mnemonics. They will turbo-charge your memorizing ability, and, together with this book, constitute a formidable arsenal for your mental performance.

If you have any questions or would like more information on other tips on memory improvement or future book releases, you can write to info@ImproveYourMemoryToday.net or visit www.ImproveYourMemoryToday.net. I'll be looking forward to hearing from you! In the meantime, take care, and good luck with whatever you will do with your improved memory!

Thomas C. Randall

Appendix

List of Mind Mapping Software

Software	Platforms	Notes/Features
3D Topicscape	Windows	Desktop application that presents Mind Maps as a 3d scene where each node is a cone. Imports MindManager, Personal Brain, FreeMind, text and folders.
Buzan's iMindMap	Windows, Mac OS X, Linux	Desktop application that provides organic Mind Mapping methods to create Maps for brainstorming, organizing, creative thinking, project management and planning. Integrates with Microsoft Office, OpenOffice.org and iWork.
Creately	Cross-platform	Online Adobe Flash-based diagramming and visual thinking tool for collaboration. Diagramming software with Mind Map capability.
Inspiration	Mac OS X, Windows, Palm	Visual Learning, Mind Mapping
LucidChart	Web application	An HTML5-based collaborative diagramming tool that can be used for both Mind Mapping and concept

The Quick and Easy Guide to Mind Map

Software	Platforms	Notes/Features
		mapping
Microsoft Visio	Windows	Part of Microsoft Office family of products, it can draw nearly any static diagram including block diagrams, organizational charts, maps, plans or workflows.
Mind42	Web application	Browser-based collaborative web application; real-time collaborative editing (the application name, "Mind42," is intended to be read as "Mind for two"); free to use without functional limitations; limited support by developer.
MindGenius	Windows	Different mapping views for brainstorming, planning, project management, and presentations; advanced categories, analysis and task management functionality
MindManager	Windows, Mac OS X	Desktop application comes in Basic and Pro versions. Integrated with Microsoft Office, available Gantt chart add-in, built-in spreadsheet, Fluent UI.
Mind Mapper	Windows	• Process Flow, Org Charts, Fishbone diagramming • Concept maps and Flowcharts • Built-in Presentation • Post it style memo notes • Integrates with Microsoft Office
MindMeister	Windows, Mac OS X, Linux	• Browser-based collaborative web application • Offline Mode • Android, iPhone and iPad applications, providing access to online Mind Maps • Built-in chat • Subscription based, also

74

Appendix

Software	Platforms	Notes/Features
		offering a free limited access option
MindView	Windows, Mac OS X	• Professional Microsoft Office Integration (Word, PowerPoint, Excel, Microsoft Outlook, Project) • 6 Interchangeable Views – Including Gantt Chart and Timeline • Calculation Feature and Excel Integration • Optimized for Project Management • Advanced Filter Function
NovaMind	Mac OS X, Windows	One of the only programs that has a free layout mode where you can put the branches where you like.)
PersonalBrain	Windows, Mac OS X, Unix, Unix-like	Graphically intensive and customizable GUI, extremely cross-platform. Notes, calendar, Microsoft Outlook features. Multiple parent node capability.
Qiqqa	Windows	Minds maps for academics oriented around their research papers, notes and annotations.
SmartDraw	Windows	SmartDraw is a visual processor used to create flowcharts, organization charts, Mind Maps, Gantt charts, and other visuals.
SpicyNodes	Adobe Flash	radial maps, viewer can move from node to node
Visual Mind	Windows	Supports collaboration (client/server) mode.
XMind Pro	Windows, Mac OS X, Linux	

Reference

Toi, H (2009), *Research on how Mind Map improves Memory*. Paper presented at the International Conference on Thinking, Kuala Lumpur, 22nd to 26th June 2009.

Al-Jarf, R. (2009),*Enhancing Freshman students' Writing Skills with a Mind Mapping software*. Paper presented at the 5th International Scientific Conference, eLearning and Software for Education, Bucharest, April 2009.

Mento, A. J., Martinelli, P. and Jones R. M. (1999), *Mind Mapping in Executive Education: Applications and Outcomes*. The Journal of Management Development, Vol. 18, Issue 4.

Zampetakis, L. A., Tsironis, L. and Moustakis, V. (2007), *Creativity Development in Engineering Education: The Case of Mind Mapping*. Journal of Management Development, Vol. 26, No. 4, pp 370-380.

Mueller, A., Johnston, M. and Bligh, D. (2002), *Joining Mind Mapping and Care Planning to Enhance Student Critical Thinking and Achieve Holistic Nursing Care*. Nursing Diagnosis, 13, 1, pg. 24.

Goodnough, K. and Woods, R. (2002), *Student and Teacher Perceptions of Mind Mapping: A Middle School Case Study* Paper presented at the Annual Meeting of American Educational Research Association, New Orleans, 1st to 5th April 2002.

Appendix

Ralston, J. and Cook, D. (2007), *Collaboration, ICT and Mind Mapping.* Reflecting Education, Vol. 3, No. 1, pp 61-73.

For more information, visit
www.ImproveYourMemoryToday.net
email: info@ImproveYourMemoryToday.net

To leave a review, go to
www.ImproveYourMemoryToday.net/review_MM

Also from the author:

The Quick and Easy Guide to Memory Improvement: 45 Practical Tips You Can Use to Boost Your Memory
(details: improveyourmemorytoday.net/book)
The Quick and Easy Guide to Mnemonics: Improve Your Memory Instantly with 15 Powerful Memory Aids
(details: improveyourmemorytoday.net/book2)

Made in the USA
Lexington, KY
02 March 2013